Search for a Living Fossil

The Story of the Coelacanth

by ELEANOR CLYMER

Illustrated by JERRY ROBINSON

Published by Scholastic Book Services, a division
of Scholastic Magazines, Inc., New York, N. Y.

Single copy price 45¢. Quantity prices available on request.

1st printing . . . . January 1966

Printed in the U.S.A.

Scientists were startled more than a hundred years ago by the discovery in England of a 250-million-year-old fossil fish. Such a fossil had never before been brought to their attention. The ancient fish had strange leglike fins that were supported by hollow spines. Louis Agassiz, the great Swiss geologist, named it *coelacanth* (SEE-la-kanth) after two Greek words meaning "hollow" and "spine."

Contents

Preface

THIS IS A BOOK ABOUT A FISH. It is a big fish with steel-blue scales, a fish so strange that the old fisherman who saw it lying on the deck of a boat thought it didn't look like a fish at all.

Scientists said it was incredible. Museum directors insisted it must be a mistake. Crowds lined up to stare at it.

Why so much excitement over a fish?

Fish have always fascinated people. They come from that mysterious world below the water, of which, even now, we know so very little.

They are so marvelously made, so beautifully adapted to the water in which they move, breathe, and live. There are so many kinds of fish — all so different and surprising. If we could only go down and walk or float about among them! People have always wanted to do that, just as they have always wanted to fly like the birds.

Until a few years ago, human beings could no more do one than the other. All they could do was to stand on the shore and gather the scraps that the waves washed up. Or they could sail on the surface and peer down a few feet into the shining green water. Or they could let down their nets and lines to catch the creatures that might be passing by.

The sea was great and terrible. It frightened men with its power. It inspired them with its beauty. And always it stirred their imagination. So people invented wonderful stories about that unknown world. They imagined cities under the ocean, sirens that sang wonderful songs to weary sailors, monster whales as big as islands, with trees on their backs, and sea serpents that could coil themselves around a ship and crush it to splinters. There were sea gods that could stir up the waves and had to be appeased with gifts. There were talking fish that could grant wishes.

Some of these things were pure imagination, others were based on reality. Some have been explained, others still defy explanation.

Sirens are supposed to have been dugongs or sea-cows (big whiskered mammals like hippopotamuses with flippers), an explanation not very flattering to human females. As for sea serpents, every few years there is a report of an enormous creature with a long neck, which has been seen swimming in the sea. These reports have come from all sorts of people — farmers and fishermen as well as scientists — and therefore it is not safe to say they are pure imagination. Someday the mystery will be solved.

Today, of course, with modern diving gear, men can actually explore beneath the surface of the sea and photograph the fishes on their native heath. With modern instruments, they can measure the depth of the ocean and find the temperature of the water. They can draw maps of the sea bottom.

Even so, the ocean is unbelievably vast and it is

still very mysterious. And every so often, even now, a fisherman's net sweeps the bottom and brings up something quite real, but almost as incredible as any magic fish that ever talked.

This is the story of one of those strange creatures. It is also the story of determination and perseverance — the determination of a man of science who set himself a task and persevered until it was accomplished.

Chapter 1

A Strange Fish

On December 22, 1938, a fishing boat commanded by one Captain Goosen came to port in East London, a seacoast town in South Africa. All kinds of ships docked in the harbor — ships taking on fruit and vegetables and grain from the farms, gold from the mines; ships bringing in goods from all over the world and, most important, fish from the ocean. The Indian Ocean, off the east coast of South Africa, teemed with all kinds of sea life. The East London market supplied fish for most of the country.

But this time, for some reason, the catch had not been good. Captain Goosen had been out for several days, sweeping the fishing grounds with his big net. At last he decided to head for port. On the way, the trawler passed the mouth of the Chalumna River.

"Should we have a try here?" the captain wondered.

Usually this was not a good place for fishing. It was not deep — about forty fathoms (240 feet) — and the bottom was rocky and rough. Fishermen did not like to trawl here, for the jagged rocks could ruin a net. However, the captain didn't like to go back without a full load. He decided to risk it.

The net was cast again and the ship trawled in a big ellipse, about three miles offshore. This time they were lucky.

They got about a ton and a half of fish that could be sold for food. They also got a couple of tons of sharks, which would be used for fertilizer. The winches pulled up the net. The rope at the bottom of the net was jerked, and the whole silvery, struggling mass of fish was dumped on the deck. Then the ship made for the home port, full steam ahead.

As the trawler steamed homeward, the deck hands sorted the catch. The edible fish were put on one side, the sharks and the unusable creatures on another.

Almost at the bottom of the heap, buried under tons of fish, the men found a large fish with steel-blue scales. None of them had ever seen one like it. What could it be?

"Better call the captain," somebody said.

The captain came. He poked at the monster. It heaved itself up, snapping its great jaws, and almost caught his hand.

The captain jumped back. "Put it over to one side," he ordered. "We'll save it for the museum."

The creature lay on the deck, heaving and panting. All the other fish were dead by this time. And this one had been on the bottom of the heap! Only a few sharks had been known to survive such treatment. But the great blue fish continued to gasp for hours. At last it died.

It was a blazing hot day, though the calendar said it was December; for this was the southern hemisphere, where the winter months are hot and June, July, and August are cold and rainy. As the ship steamed on through the sunny afternoon, the cargo began to smell rather strong. At last they tied up at the dock. The captain went ashore. He stopped in at the office of his company and asked the clerk to telephone the East London Museum, to say a trawler had just come in.

"I'll be right there," said the curator.

The curator of the East London Museum was a young woman whose name was Miss M. C. Courtenay-Latimer.

She was quite accustomed to being summoned down to the dock to rummage through piles of dead fish. It was an unusual occupation for a woman, but Miss Latimer was an unusual young woman.

Many towns in South Africa had museums — small places that displayed local curiosities, such as frontier costumes, guns, tools, cooking utensils. It was not so long since South Africans had been busy settling the country, subduing the natives who lived there, plowing the land to make farms. Their descendants were interested mainly in preserving reminders of local human history.

Miss Latimer's little museum was young and poor. But she was young too, and full of ideas. She had decided to make her museum one of the best in the country. She was going to have more in it than Uncle Joost's gun and Aunt Millie's best dress. She planned to specialize in science.

But how could she do that when the board of directors would not give her any money to work with?

There was so little money that she didn't even have a staff. She herself was the whole staff, with only one assistant, whose name was Enoch.

The board of directors did not think much of her idea for a scientific museum. The people of East London were not interested in science, and why should the museum spend money on something the public didn't care about?

As a matter of fact, there were few trained scientists in South Africa at that time. When a fossil or a strange plant or an animal of real scientific interest was found, the usual procedure was to send it to Europe, where the experts were and where it could be shown to people who mattered!

Miss Latimer thought the people of East London mattered, and she thought that the best way to get them excited about their museum was to show them things they were interested in. And the people of East London were interested in *fish*.

Not only was the town a fishing port, but fishing was the local hobby. Everybody went fishing. Everybody talked about fish. Everybody wanted to see new and strange kinds of fish.

So she made an arrangement with the big fishing

companies. They were to let her know when the boats came in, and were to save anything unusual that they would otherwise throw away. Therefore she was not surprised when the office telephoned her.

She called a taxi, gathered up some old sacks for her specimens, and with her assistant, Enoch, she hurried down to the docks.

The trawlermen greeted her. They liked the lady who came down to the ship to poke through piles of dead fish and who didn't seem to mind how badly they smelled.

"Over here, miss," said an old trawlerman, leading her to the heap they had put aside for her.

As she expected, most of the fish were sharks. She already had specimens of all of them. There did not seem to be anything of interest this time. She was about to depart when she saw the strange fish that had been at the bottom of the pile. It was a big fish with heavy, steel-blue scales. She had never seen scales like those before.

The men pulled it out for her. For a while, all she could do was stand there and stare at it. She had never seen anything like it. The fish was five feet long. It had a huge mouth with vicious-looking teeth. Its tail was big and fleshy, with a fringe of fins at the end, and with a little bit of an extra tail sticking out of the middle of it. But the strangest thing about the fish was its fins. They looked more like legs or flippers than fins.

"Have you ever seen a fish like that before?" she asked.

"No, miss," said the man. "Not in thirty years at sea. Looks more like a lizard than a fish, doesn't it?"

It certainly did look like a cross between a fish and a lizard.

"I don't know what it is," she said, "but I must have it for the museum."

"Captain thought you'd want it," said the man. "Good thing it's dead, though. When we hauled it in, it snapped them jaws terrible. Captain went to poke it like, and it heaved up and snapped at him and almost got his hand. That's something for Miss Latimer, Captain said."

Miss Latimer was grateful. But how was she going to get it to the museum. It was a hot day, and the fish smelled. It had a peculiar smell — worse than any other fish she had ever handled. Maybe it was from the oil that seemed to ooze from it.

She asked the men to weigh it for her. It weighed 127 pounds.

"Put it in the taxi, please," she said to the driver.

"Oh no, miss, not in my taxi!" said the driver.

She showed him that she had pieces of canvas to put on the floor, but the taximan kept shaking his head.

At last, after much pleading and coaxing, she got him to agree to take it, but he wouldn't touch the monster himself. Miss Latimer and Enoch struggled with it and managed to haul it into the taxi. Off they went to the museum. Then they had to haul the fish out of the taxi.

Now the question was, what to do with it? Where could they keep it? In a big enough tank, with plenty of preservative, it might keep. But the museum had no tank. In this heat the fish had already begun to spoil. The odor was terrible.

She was beginning to wonder whether she should bother to keep it at all. Perhaps first she should try to find out what it was.

She went to her books and tried to look it up. She pored through every book on living fishes that she could find. Not a single one mentioned such a fish as this.

In that case, she reasoned, it must be something rare and she must keep it. But it couldn't stay in the museum in this condition. She must get it to the taxidermist and have it preserved.

First she made some notes. She drew pictures of the fish, measured it, and noted its peculiar scales — great thick ones, each scale fitting into a socket twice as deep as its own length. The head was covered with bony plates. Strangest of all were the leglike fins and the heavy tail with the tiny extra tail in the middle.

She asked a friend who had a camera to take some pictures. Finally she and Enoch loaded the heavy, slimy creature on a hand truck, which she had to borrow, since the museum had none of its own. Together they pushed it to the taxidermist's.

Of course mounting a fish meant cutting out all the soft inside parts, and if this fish was unusual, the soft parts would be important. She begged the taxidermist to keep everything he removed.

Then she went to have a talk with the chairman of the museum's board of directors, to tell him what she had done.

The chairman was not much interested. What was so important about this fish? Why was she so excited about it? She couldn't explain precisely, but she felt sure that it was important. Very well then, they would pay to have it mounted. But that was all they would do. The board certainly would not spend any money on research.

That reply was not enough for Miss Latimer. She had worked hard. She had carried home a large smelly fish, had taken the responsibility for it, and she wanted to know more about it. Who could tell her? There was only one person: Dr. Smith!

Chapter 2

J. L. B. Smith to the Rescue

DR. JAMES L. B. SMITH was a professor at the University of Grahamstown, about a hundred miles from East London. Officially he was a professor of chemistry. But that was only half his life. The other half was fish!

When Dr. Smith was a little boy, his family used to go to a lovely holiday place on a river, some distance from the sea, called Knysna.* Here there were great

* Say: NIZ-na.

trees full of birds, mysterious swamps, and trails through the wilderness. Best of all, there were calm lagoons where strange and beautiful fish swam about.

One day James's father gave him an old rod and line, and they went fishing together. The father showed the boy how to bait the hook and drop it into the water. They waited. Suddenly the line bobbed. Something down there below the calm surface was pulling on it. The little boy pulled too. The line whipped into the air. At the end of it was a struggling, silvery fish — his very first fish. From that moment fishing was James Smith's greatest pleasure, but not just catching fish. He had to know all about them — their names, how they were made, how they lived.

As he grew up, he studied all the books he could find. But there were not many books he could use. Most of them were so technical that they could only be understood by experts. He wanted to be an expert, but he wasn't one yet.

So he made up his own system. He wrote down descriptions of all the fishes he caught. He drew pictures of them, although he wasn't much of an artist.

Then he started collecting fishes up and down the South African coast. To his surprise, he found that no-

body had done this before, and that he was doing pioneer work. The fishes of the Indian Ocean off South Africa were amazing creatures, marvels of beauty or fascinatingly ugly.

Dr. Smith couldn't spend his whole time with fish. He had to earn his living, and he did it by teaching chemistry at Grahamstown. Chemistry was a subject more in demand than ichthyology, the study of fish. But every minute he could spare from his classes was given over to fish. Soon he was publishing papers about fish, and people were coming to him with new kinds that they had caught and could not identify. He was helping commercial fishermen as well as amateurs, by classifying fish and explaining their habits.

He had to work very hard to keep up with his two interests. But he did it. He went out in fishing vessels with the crews, braving bad weather and seasickness for the chance to look over the "rubbish" that they couldn't use and would throw overboard. He went to remote places to talk to farmers and fishermen and lighthousekeepers.

He worked with the curators of museums, and at many of them he was Honorary Curator of Fishes.

He also became interested in paleontology, the

study of life in past ages. He studied fossils as well as living fishes, and in his spare moments, when he had time to dream, he dreamed of someday discovering something very rare and marvelous — perhaps a sea serpent or some other creature that would amaze the scientific world.

By 1938, J. L. B. Smith was the best-known ichthyologist in the country. He was an authority on African fishes. And so it was to him that Miss Latimer decided to write.

Dr. Smith and his young wife (they had been married only a few months) were spending the Christmas holidays at their house at Knysna, about 250 miles from Grahamstown. The professor had been looking forward to this holiday for a long time. He was a slight, high-strung man; he worked very hard, and he was desperately tired.

It was peaceful here. There was no telephone closer than the neighborhood shop. The post office was in the village, and even the mail didn't come regularly. The roads were terrible. Very few people traveled over them, and the Smiths did not expect many visitors. In a few days there would be examination papers to correct, but for the present there was nothing to do but fish in the lagoon and work in the laboratory — Dr. Smith's favorite forms of relaxation.

In the midst of this peace and quiet, something happened that was like a bomb exploding.

On January 3, 1939, a friend came to see them, bringing a stack of mail that had been piling up at the post office. Dr. and Mrs. Smith sat down to read it. There were Christmas cards, bills, letters from friends, and as always some letters asking for help in identifying fish.

He picked up one from the East London Museum. He knew Miss Latimer's handwriting well. He opened the letter. This is what he read:

East London,
South Africa.
23rd December 1938

Dear Dr. Smith,

I had the most queer-looking specimen brought to notice yesterday. The captain of the trawler told me about it, so I immediately set off to see the specimen, which I had removed to our taxidermist as soon as I could. I however have drawn a very rough sketch, and am in hopes that you may be able to assist me in classing it.

It is coated in heavy scales, almost armorlike, the fins resemble limbs, and are scaled right up to a fringe of filament. The spinous dorsal has tiny white spines down each filament. Note drawing inked in red.

I would be so pleased if you could let me know what you think, though I know just how difficult it is from a description of this kind.

Wishing you all happiness for the season.

Yours sincerely,
M. Courtenay-Latimer

It seemed like a routine request. Then Dr. Smith turned the page and looked at the picture. He stared at it. He had never seen such a thing in all his life. A fish with legs! His first thought was that this was some kind of ridiculous mistake. Miss Latimer must have taken leave of her senses. Or maybe it was a joke. But no. Miss Latimer was a very careful, serious young woman. It would not be like her to play jokes.

Then he thought she might have made a mistake in her drawing. And yet . . . and yet . . . somewhere he *had* seen such a fish. But where? Not in the sea. Not on the deck of a boat. No — wait . . . Now he had it: in a book — a book on fossil fish! This was the picture of a fossil fish, anywhere from 70 to 300 million years old! Miss Latimer had sent him a picture of a coelacanth! *

But this was impossible. The letter distinctly said it had been caught in the waters off South Africa.

He stared at the picture. It looked exactly like the reconstructions of fossil fish he had seen. If she had sent him a picture of a living dinosaur, he could not have been more astounded.

Suddenly he realized that his wife was staring at him anxiously. "What on earth is the matter?" she asked.

Dr. Smith looked up in surprise. He had quite forgotten that there was anybody else in the room.

"I have a letter from Miss Latimer," he said. "She wants me to identify a fish."

"What is wrong with that?" Mrs. Smith asked.

Dr. Smith shook his head. "Don't think me crazy," he said, "but this is a type of fish that has been extinct for millions of years."

"Are you sure? How do you know?" his wife demanded.

"Look at that picture," he said. "Look at the tail.

---

* Say: SEE-la-kanth.

Look at the fins and the plates on the head, and the scales."

Suddenly he made up his mind. "I must see that fish at once. I can't be sure of anything until I have examined it. I'll have to go to East London right away."

"But how can you possibly do that?" Mrs. Smith asked.

She was right. East London was 350 miles away, over dreadful roads. Trains were few and far between. Today, with good roads, in a modern car, it would be a trip of a few hours. In a plane, perhaps an hour. But in 1938, in South Africa, such a journey would take several days. And in a few days he would have to start work on his examination papers. That was his job, and it came first. He could not put it off in order to go and look at a fish that might or might not be something unusual.

"Well, I'll have to have the fish sent here," he said. "That will be the best way. Then I can work on it in the laboratory."

His wife looked at the letter. "Do you see when this letter was written?" she said. "It may be too late."

He had an unpleasant shock. The letter was dated December 23. And this was the third of January.

What must Miss Latimer be thinking? She had expected to hear from him at once. Why, the fish might be completely spoiled by now! What had the taxidermist done with it? Had he thrown away the insides? Had he, at least, saved the gills and the skeleton?

"I'll telephone her at once," said Dr. Smith.

He rushed to the neighborhood shop.

"I must make a long-distance call at once," he said to the operator.

Then he had another unpleasant shock. It was not a simple matter to make a long-distance call. In fact, he was to find out that nothing in connection with this fish was going to be simple.

It was now one o'clock in the afternoon. The call could not possibly be put through before five. At five, the museum would be closed for the day, and Miss Latimer had no telephone at home.

It seems queer to us, for whom a telephone is as much a part of a household as the kitchen sink. But that was South Africa in 1938.

The shopkeeper was concerned. Was anyone sick or dying? — No, it was nothing like that. — In that case, why was Dr. Smith so upset?

Dr. Smith didn't stop to explain. He rushed off to the

village. If he couldn't telephone, he could at least send a telegram. The telegram emphasized what to him was of vital necessity:

> MOST IMPORTANT PRESERVE SKELETON AND GILLS FISH DESCRIBED

For even if the soft parts were destroyed or decayed, a great deal could be learned from the bones.

He arranged for a telephone call to be put through next day and rushed home to write a letter. His heart pounded, his brain was in a whirl.

A coelacanth! A living fossil! The more he thought about it, the more he wanted to believe that it *was* one. All his life he had secretly longed to make some great discovery, something that nobody else in the world had ever done. Perhaps now his dream was coming true. But it would not do to be too hopeful.

He wrote to Miss Latimer. He tore up the letter and wrote another. His sandy hair stood up on his head. His wife hovered anxiously, trying to help. At last he managed to write a letter that was just right, calm but enthusiastic. He was interested in her news, he said. What she had found seemed to resemble an extinct fish, and she was to take very good care of it, at least until he could examine it and make sure just what it was.

Then, somehow, he managed to get through the rest of the day and night. Morning came at last. He rushed off to the shop. Then he had to wait three long hours before the call came through. At last he heard Miss Latimer's voice.

He was almost afraid to ask what had happened to the fish's insides, but he managed to stammer out his question. His heart sank when he heard the answer. Yes, they had been thrown away. It was impossible to keep them. The garbage wagon had taken them away.

Dr. Smith was desperate. He would take a plane to East London and dig through the rubbish with his own hands. But it was too late. The garbage had been dumped far out at sea.

At last he finished talking and hung up, and turned to pay for the call. It cost several pounds. Everyone in the shop was amazed. They had all been standing there, drinking in every word and waiting to learn whether someone in the professor's family had died. But the call had been about a dead fish!

It was plain to see what those villagers thought of

a man who would pay so much money to talk about a dead fish. He was obviously not quite right in the head.

Dr. Smith was inclined to agree with them. After all, he was jumping to conclusions on the basis of one tiny sketch. He was behaving quite unlike a serious scientist. He had to have books to verify his conclusions. But there were no books on fossil fishes at Knysna. He sent off a telegram to a friend at the museum in Cape Town, the largest in the country.

Two more agonizing days passed, and the book arrived. It was Volume II of the *Catalogue of Fossil Fishes of the British Museum.* With shaking fingers he opened it. There could be no doubt. What Miss Latimer had found must be a coelacanth, though every paleontologist in the world would swear that the last coelacanth had died 70 million years ago!

Somehow, unknown to the human race, coelacanths had survived all this time and were alive somewhere in the ocean. For if one had been found, there must be others.

Why had nobody ever seen one before? It was too big a fish to be invisible.

That raised another question: why was it so big?

The fossil coelacanth had been a little fish, about a foot long — never more than twenty inches.

However, in 70 million years, the little fish might have evolved into a big one. And if its outside appearance was so much like that of the fossil, perhaps its inner parts were too. How exciting this was! Think what it would mean to scientists to study not just the bones and teeth of a fossil, but the nervous system, the breathing apparatus, the stomach, the brain, and the muscles!

He was so wrought up that he couldn't eat, couldn't sleep. The holiday that was to have been so restful was no holiday. It was torture.

The examination papers arrived. It was all he could do to work on them. He could not leave until they were finished.

He wrote to Miss Latimer again. Please, he begged, please try to remember all you can about the fish. What was its air bladder like? Had she remembered to have the skull and the jawbones preserved intact? He would need to know how the jaw was attached to the skull. Had they kept any other parts of the skeleton? Were the gills preserved, so that he could learn how the animal breathed? Could she perhaps send him the skin?

On the ninth of January a letter arrived, dated the fourth. (It always seemed to take at least six days for a letter to arrive in Knysna.) The specimen was being mounted and looked very well, Miss Latimer said. As for the skeleton, there *wasn't* any.

> . . . The backbone was a column of soft white gristle-like material, running from skull to tail — this was an inch across and filled with oil, which spouted out as cut through. The flesh was plastic, and could be worked like clay. The stomach was empty . . .
>
> The gills had small rows of fine spines, but were unfortunately thrown away with the body.
>
> Mr. Center has almost mounted the specimen now, and is not doing it badly at all — the oil is still pouring out from the skin, which seems to have oil cells beneath each scale.
>
> The scales are armorlike, fitting into deep pockets . . .

Poor Miss Latimer was very unhappy.

> . . . I have done every possible thing to preserve and not lose any points, and feel worried to think in the end I allowed the body and gills to be discarded. They were kept for three days, and when I did not hear from you I gave the order for disposal.

Dr. Smith wondered whether Miss Latimer and the

trawler captain could have been mistaken. Perhaps they hadn't caught a live fish after all. Maybe it was just a fossil that had been preserved in the ocean in some way. Then he remembered that the fish had tried to bite the captain's hand. No, dead fossils didn't bite.

He wrote again. Please, he asked, offer a reward for another specimen. And be sure to have a large tank ready in case one should be found. He even told her how to make the tank! The fish was to be preserved in strong formalin solution. He would pay for everything. And please, if possible, send him a photograph and one of the scales to examine.

Alas, all the photographs had been spoiled. But Miss Latimer did manage to send him three scales. This was a ray of sunshine. The scales were almost exactly like those of the fossil fish. He decided to name the fish *Latimeria*, in honor of Miss Latimer.

At long last his examination papers were done, and he and his wife could start for East London. By this time the rainy season had begun. The roads were flooded, and it was the middle of February before they got there.

Dr. Smith was in such a state of excitement that he did not stop for anything. He rushed to the museum.

He saw no one and nothing except the fish he had come so far to examine. There it was, mounted, its mouth open, its fins more like legs than anything else. He put out his hand and touched it gently. There was no more doubt in his mind. It was a coelacanth!

Chapter 3

A Look at Our Beginnings

WHY WAS THIS "LIVING FOSSIL" SO IMPORTANT? And why was Dr. Smith so excited about it? To answer these questions, one must know something about fossils.

What Is a Fossil?

The word *fossil* comes from a Latin word meaning "to dig." It used to mean anything that was dug up out of the earth. Then the word came to mean the remains of any living thing that had been preserved in the earth in one way or another. Now it refers to something very, very old.

Usually when a living thing dies, its body decays. The organism vanishes from sight and becomes part of the earth from which it came. But sometimes, though rarely, something else happens.

How Are Fossils Made?

Let us think of a fish that lived in the water near the mouth of a river. When it died, it sank to the bottom and was covered with sediment — mud washed down by the river.

The soft parts of the fish decayed, but the bones, being harder, remained long enough to leave an imprint in the mud. More sediment was washed down — tons of it, in the course of the centuries. The weight of all that sediment on the mud turned it to rock. Millions of years passed. The crust of the earth, shifting and buckling, rose up out of the sea, and the waters drew back. What was once sea bottom was now dry land. People digging there broke open the rock and found the imprint of the fish.

This is one way in which fossils are made. There

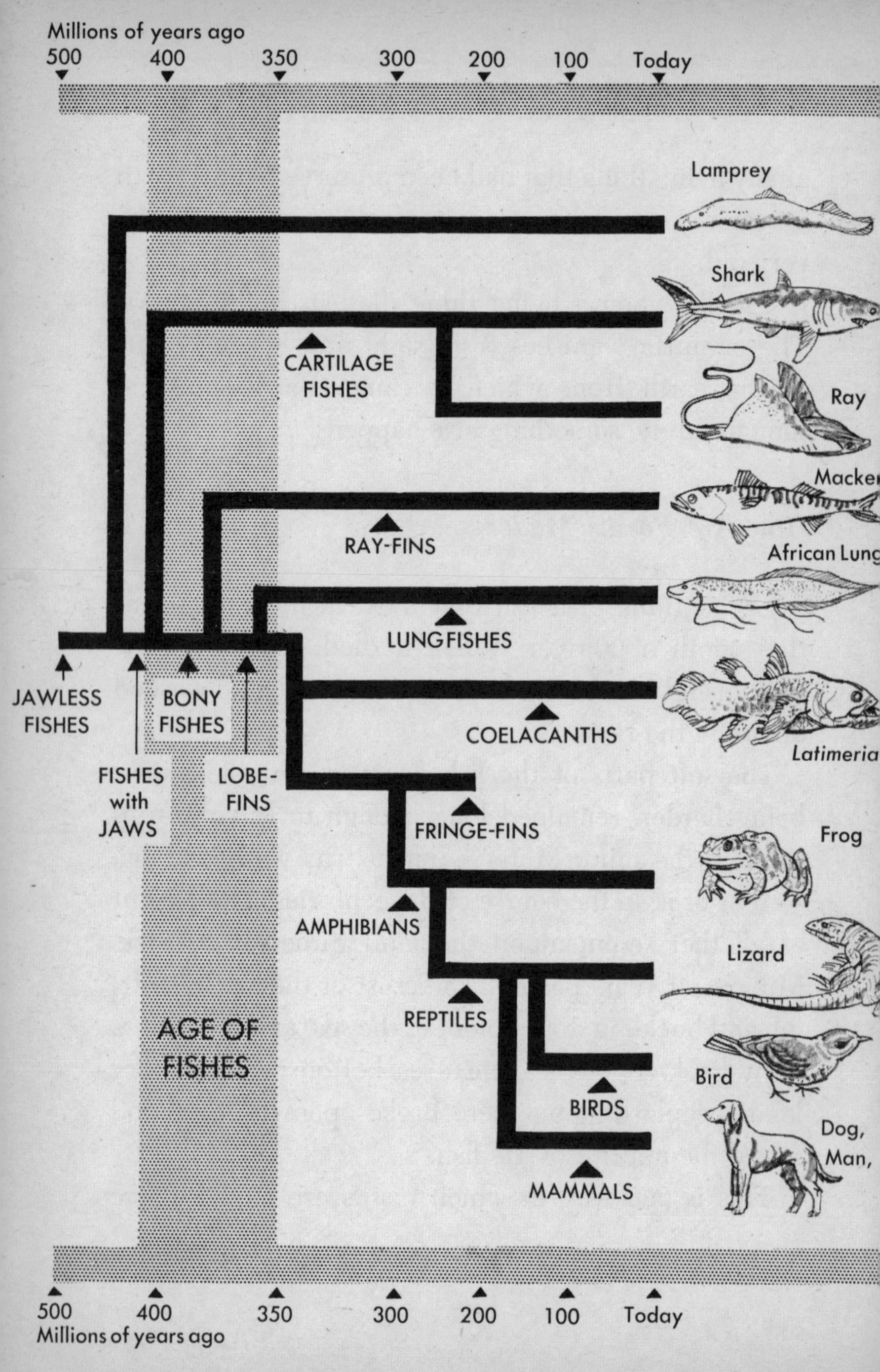
Millions of years ago
500
400
350
300
200
100
Today
Lamprey
Shark
CARTILAGE FISHES
Ray
RAY-FINS
LUNG FISHES
COELACANTHS
Latimeria
FRINGE-FINS
Frog
AMPHIBIANS
Lizard
REPTILES
Bird
BIRDS
Dog, Man,
MAMMALS
JAWLESS FISHES
FISHES with JAWS
BONY FISHES
LOBE-FINS
AGE OF FISHES
500
400
350
300
200
100
Today
Millions of years ago

are others. Sometimes the preserved bones themselves are found. Mud seeped into the tiny spaces within them and hardened there, so that the bone seems actually to be turned to stone.

Sometimes the skeleton is so clearly outlined that we can see where the soft parts were; sometimes, rarely, the soft parts themselves have left an imprint — almost a shadow in the rock.

Fossils are formed in other ways too. Sometimes remains are preserved by the dry air and drifting sands of the desert. Sometimes the water of a bog or the freezing cold of the Arctic keeps flesh or bone or wood from decaying. But most fossils are found in rocks, and they tell an amazing story — the history of living things.

What Does the Fossil Record Show?

The fossil record shows how the ancestors of today's creatures were shaped millions of years ago. It shows many species that have since died out. It also leaves many gaps in our knowledge that we must fill in by guesswork.

The biggest gap is at the beginning. The first living creatures had soft bodies, and when they died, their bodies decayed and were lost. We can guess that they were like the soft-bodied creatures living today: one-celled animals; simple many-celled animals, such as sponges and jellyfish and worms.

Then arose two very different groups of animals.

In one group were creatures with no skeletons inside their bodies, but with hard *outer* shells. And here we begin to have evidence from the fossil record. In the rocks of some 600 million years ago, we find the beginnings of hard-shelled creatures. They multiplied into thousands of kinds: some looking like strange snails, others like clams; sea lilies, which still exist in some parts of the ocean; enormous numbers of animals that were the forerunners of shrimps, lobsters, spiders, and insects; sea scorpions with fierce jaws, some of them growing to huge sizes.

The other group slowly changed into the one that we ourselves belong to: the vertebrates, animals with a bony skeleton *inside* the body. And these internal skeletons left fossil records too.

The First Vertebrates

The first trace of animals with backbones is found in rocks 480 million years old — rocks which were once the bottom of the sea, but were pushed upward when the earth's crust buckled and folded. In those rocks, we have found the remains of a particular kind of fish. These fishes were only a few inches long. Their heads and bodies were covered with bony plates, which perhaps protected them from the terrible sea scorpions. But more important, they had a stiff inner skeleton made of gristle or cartilage.

These fishes had no jaws. They had round mouths which sucked in the mud from the sea bottom, and gills which strained out food and took in oxygen. They had eyes, and a nostril for smelling. They had no paired side fins and probably were not very good at swimming. But they were the first real vertebrates, the first animals with backbones. From such ancestors came all the rest of the vertebrates.

Millions of years passed, and by then fishes had jaws and fins. They spread from the seas into the rivers. They found many new foods to eat — plants and other animals. They became better swimmers, better at escaping from their enemies, and also better at catching their food. They filled the waters of the earth. In the rocks formed 420 to 350 million years ago, there are so many fossil fishes that we call this period the Age of Fishes.

In time there were two general kinds of fishes. One kind had lost its bony plates, keeping its inside skeleton of cartilage. These fish became the ancestors of our present-day sharks.

The other kind, the bony fishes, became the ancestors of all the other fishes of the world — and also the ancestors of all other vertebrates, including man.

How did this come about? As the result of two new parts in the fish body: side fins and *lungs!*

The First Lungs

Why should fish need lungs? Most fish get their oxygen from the water as it passes over the gills. The gills are fringes of flesh with many tiny blood vessels close to the surface. The oxygen in the water passes through the thin walls of these blood vessels and into the fish's body.

In the period from 400 to 280 million years ago, the climate in much of the world was like that of the tropics today. It was warm and humid. There were many swamps. Plants grew in them, and there were plenty of insects and spiders. Many fish lived in the rivers, but tropical rivers are undependable. Sometimes there were floods. At other times the rivers would be stagnant and shallow. The water, full of decaying plants, would become too poisonous for fish to breathe. Fish could live there only if they had some way to get oxygen. The lung was the answer.

The lung began as a pocket in the wall of the fish's gullet. The fish swallowed water, air, and food down its gullet. Air was trapped in the pocket, and the pocket became a *swim bladder* that helped the fish to float. Then something new happened. Oxygen from the air passed into the lining of the swim bladder and was absorbed into the blood of the fish. When this happened, the swim bladder became a lung.

Not all swim bladders, however, became lungs. By about 380 or 390 million years ago, the bony fishes of the world had become divided into two groups: the ray-finned and the lobe-finned. The *ray-finned* fishes kept their swim bladders. These fishes were the ancestors of all the bony fishes we know today.

It was among the *lobe-finned* fishes that lungs appeared. Some, the *lungfishes,* became very widespread. Their fossils are found all over the world. Then they dwindled to a small group that still exists today. There are several kinds, but the best known is the African lungfish, or Kamongo, as the Africans call it.

Kamongo lives in swamps and rivers. When there is plenty of water, it swims about and breathes through gills like any other fish. When the water dries up, it digs itself into the mud, leaving a tube for an airshaft. It goes to sleep there, taking a breath through the tube about once an hour. The mud can dry up and bake in the sun, and the fish will still go on sleeping. It can sleep there seven years if necessary. When the rain comes and the mud dissolves, the fish wakes up and goes about its business.

People have dug up Kamongo in a lump of clay, packed it in a tin can, and shipped it off to museums in Europe and America. When the can is opened and the clay is put into water, the fish wakes up, as good as new.

The lungfishes are interesting as "living fossils." They have survived for more than 350 million years. It would be hard to decide whether they are a "success" or not. If merely staying alive from one rainy spell to the next is success, then they are successful.

Another group of lobe-finned fishes, closely related to the lungfish, was that known as the *fringe-fins.* They too were air-breathing, but the most striking thing about these fish was that their fins were built like stumpy legs, with fringes at the ends. The fleshy fins were attached to the body by a series of bones, which made them strong enough to bear the weight of the body. They were fresh-water fish; they had internal nostrils, instead of the simple pits that most fishes have. This meant that they could breathe air by coming to the surface and keeping their mouths closed, so as not to swallow water.

The First Amphibians

The fringe-fins appear to have become extinct about 200 million years ago, so perhaps they were not as successful as the lungfishes from the standpoint of survival. But before the fringe-fins died out, they showed a totally new characteristic: their fleshy fins had become *legs*. And their descendants became the first amphibians — animals that live both in water and on land.

Present-day amphibians, such as frogs and salamanders, can live out of water, but they must go back to the water to lay their eggs; and their young ones, breathing through gills, must live in water until they mature.

The First Reptiles

When the descendants of the ancient amphibians began to lay eggs with hard shells, they were able to spend their whole lives on dry land. They became the first reptiles.

The First Mammals

From reptiles were descended some hairy little creatures that looked insignificant but were really very important. They were mammals. They did not lay eggs, but bore their young alive. The mothers nursed the babies until they were able to take care of themselves. This great step forward meant that mammals could one day rule the earth, for their young would not need to be completely finished on hatching from an egg. A young mammal would have time after birth to mature and to develop its most important possession — its brain.

Where Does the Coelacanth Fit In?

One group of the fringe-fins is known as the *coelacanths.* The coelacanths were much like the other fringe-fins, except that their swim bladders never became lungs. They lived chiefly in fresh water until about 140 million years ago, when they left the rivers to live in the sea. Their fossils have been found in rocks dating up to 70 million years ago. After that, they seemed to disappear.

Scientists have described them and reconstructed them so well that Dr. Smith would have known one anywhere, even in a rough sketch on the back of a letter.

This, then, was the fish that Miss Latimer had found that hot afternoon in 1938 — a fish that might have shown what the ancestors of all four-limbed vertebrates were like. This is what the trawl had swept up from some rocky ledge deep in the green water of the Indian Ocean. And this is what Dr. Smith now saw, mounted, with its mouth open to show the fierce teeth, but alas, with its heart and brain and muscles, and even its skeleton, gone forever.

Chapter 4
Latimeria Chalumnae

WHAT SHOULD DR. SMITH DO NOW? The first and most important thing was to have an article published in a scientific journal, before any stories could appear in the newspapers. This was proper scientific procedure.

He planned to name the fish *Latimeria chalumnae Smith.* This would mean that it was named for Miss Latimer, found at Chalumna, and classified by J. L. B. Smith. To do this, he had to describe it, so that there could be no mistake as to its identity. If he didn't do it soon, there was some danger that someone else, seeing a story in a newspaper or hearing about the fish, might claim to have discovered it first and might demand the right to name it something else.

He had impressed on Miss Latimer the need for secrecy. Now he had to talk to Dr. Bruce-Bays, the chairman of the East London Museum's board of directors.

Dr. Bruce-Bays was not much impressed by the fish. He thought Miss Latimer was getting overly excited. Nor was he much impressed by Dr. Smith. Smith was a slight, harried, youthful-looking man. In the rumpled field clothes in which he had hurried to the museum, he didn't look much like a great authority on fishes. Only after the chairman heard Smith talk did he realize that here was an important scientist and that the coelacanth was an important fish.

When he was finally convinced, his next thought was to get as much publicity for the museum as possible. By all means call in the reporters and let the public view the fish.

"No, no!" cried Dr. Smith. "First the article for the scientific journal!"

But it was too late. The reporters had heard about the fish. They were so eager for a story and a picture

that Smith at last consented. He stipulated that only the East London paper was to send a journalist. The reporter promised that the story and pictures would appear only in the East London *Daily Dispatch*.

But it was impossible to keep the news in East London. Soon pictures appeared in papers all over the country — indeed all over the world.

When the citizens of East London heard that they had such a scientific treasure in their midst, they began clamoring to see the fish, and it was put on exhibit. Crowds of people lined up to file past the coelacanth. Guards kept a constant watch over it.

Dr. Smith couldn't wait to get to work on the fish. He couldn't examine it while all these ceremonies were going on, and he had to get back to his job. After much pleading, he persuaded the board of directors to let the fish be sent to him at Grahamstown.

It arrived, like a distinguished visitor, with a special police guard, and was put in a room of its own in the Smiths' house.

The family were instructed by the professor not to forget it for an instant, and indeed there was little danger that they would, for the house was immediately filled with its peculiar smell! The order was given that the house was never to be left alone and that, in case of fire, the fish was to be the first thing rescued.

At last, thought Dr. Smith, he would have peace and quiet, and he could get to work. But no! Letters and phone calls began to come. Some people told him earnestly not to be foolish—that the fish was not a coelacanth, but a rock cod with a damaged tail. Others said that if it was a coelacanth, it ought to be in the British Museum in London, and not in a remote town in South Africa.

One woman wrote to say that if he was interested in old things, she would send him a violin she had had for a long time, and he could tell her if it was worth anything.

Hundreds of people offered to send in odd fish they had caught, and one man said he had a pirate map, and offered to let Dr. Smith share the treasure with him if he would help hunt it.

It was hard to concentrate in the midst of such distractions, but Dr. Smith spent every spare minute working on the fish. He would get up at three o'clock in the morning to have more time. His wife typed his notes for him, and they saw almost no outside visitors. They had coelacanth with breakfast, lunch, and dinner. It was all a strain on Mrs. Smith, who was expecting her first baby very soon, but she gamely went on helping her husband.

At last the article for the scientific journal was done. It was sent off to the British magazine *Nature*. Then Dr. Smith settled down to write a more detailed description.

To him it was little short of a tragedy that so much of the fish had been lost. But it was no use bemoaning the fact. He determined to get all the information he could from what was left. He still had the skull and the skin. He decided to open one side of the skull. This had to be done with the greatest of care, so as not to lose the tiniest bone that might have been left by the taxidermist.

Slowly and meticulously he worked, measuring every part that he uncovered, drawing pictures and comparing them with fossil fishes. It was thrilling to see how unchanged the coelacanth was. Its skull and its scales were almost exactly like those of the fossil fishes of 70 million years ago!

All that was left of the spinal column was a short length protruding into the tail, but he could see that it was a hollow tube which became solid at the tip and contained nervelike threads. In other words, it was not a vertebral column, but a true notochord, the primitive predecessor of the spinal column.

He found a central cavity inside the front of the head which he could not account for. The brain, of course, was missing, so he could not examine it. But he did find some delicate bones, just under the skin, which the taxidermist had not removed, and which he thought were meant to carry sensory canals, filled with a fluid which helped the fish maintain its balance or warned it when it was coming close to some foreign body.

He saw that some of the bones of the head seemed much like scales, and that the teeth were very similar in structure to the little knobs on the scales and must also have developed from ancient scales.

The article he was writing was developing into a book, even though its subject was an incomplete fish. He was not nearly finished when a telegram arrived saying that the board of directors in East London wanted the fish returned to the museum at once. People were coming from all over to look at it, and it wasn't there! The museum must have it back. He pleaded for more time, and was granted another week. He worked madly to get as much done as possible.

At last the police escort arrived and took the fish back to the museum.

The Smith family breathed a sigh of relief. Though there was still an enormous amount of work to be done on the book, there was no longer the same frantic rush. Dr. Smith could relax a bit, and Mrs. Smith was able to spend some time getting clothes for the baby, who was born a few weeks later.

But after all the stress, strain, and excitement had died down, one thing remained clear. If there was one coelacanth, there must be more. And more must be found, even if they had to search all the seas for them.

Chapter 5

We Must Search the Seas

IT WAS ONE THING TO SAY, "We must search the seas," and another to know where to begin. Should Dr. Smith hire a boat and go to the place where the first coelacanth had been caught? He would have done that if he thought there was any chance of finding another one in the same place. But trawlers had been fishing there for years, and nobody had even seen a coelacanth before. This one must have been a stray.

Then where could it have strayed from? He could not very well search the entire ocean.

The ocean is enormous. It covers much more of the surface of the globe than the land does. Its area is 139 million square miles; that of the land is only about 48 million. The entire ocean (that is, all the oceans of the world, for they are all connected) contains about 330 million cubic miles of water. In some places the depth of the ocean is greater than the height of the world's highest mountain. The Marianas Trench in the Pacific Ocean is about seven miles deep, while Mount Everest is about five and a half miles high. Even more remarkable, the average depth of the ocean is more than two miles, and the average height of the land is less than half a mile — about 2,300 feet.

What lies beneath all that water? Standing on the beach, where the yellow sand slopes gently down to the blue waves, the sea looks like a great watery mystery. Actually, we have learned a good deal about it in recent years.

The beach itself is the beginning of what is called the continental shelf. In most parts of the world, the continental shelf stretches outward from the shore for about thirty miles, sloping gently downward. Where the coast is flat and low, as in Holland, for example, the continental shelf stretches out much farther. In a few places — western South America and East Africa — the coast is very steep, and the shelf too plunges steeply downward. But in general the shelf has a gradual slope and a smooth floor until it reaches a depth of about 500 feet. Then it becomes much steeper, and suddenly the bottom drops away. This is the continental slope. The sea floor is broken by deep cracks, as deep as the canyons on the land. For a hundred miles or so it drops away until it merges into the real sea bottom.

Here it is totally dark. Only the upper 200 feet are lit by the sun. Below that there is a twilight zone, and then comes the abyss where no sunlight ever penetrates.

The bottom of the sea is not flat, as it was once thought to be. It is full of hills and valleys, trenches and crags. But the crags don't look sharp or jagged. Everything is covered with a carpet of soft ooze, made up of the remains of plants and animals that lived in the sea, died, and sank to the bottom.

Incredible numbers of things live in the sea, and one might think that to find one particular fish would be an utterly impossible task. But though the ocean is very big and very wet, it is not just one large mass of water. It is made up of zones, as unlike one another as the zones on land. The creatures that live in it are as different as the Arctic fox and the red fox, the bird of paradise and the house wren.

First, there are the zones of different temperatures. Creatures that live on land, surrounded by air, have had to learn to adjust to changing temperatures, because air temperature changes quickly. It gets cool or hot at different times, and land animals adjust by shivering, curling up, hibernating, stretching, panting, growing or shedding hair, and so on.

But the temperature of water is much more constant, so fish have never needed to make such adjustments. They simply stay in water of the temperature they are adapted to. Fish that are used to cold water can't go into warm water any more than a cow can cross a barbed-wire fence. If they do, they die.

Then there is depth. The deeper the water, the less light there is. The fishes that live in shallow water are usually blue or green on top, and have white bellies. This makes them less easily seen by their enemies. Those that live farther down are darker in color all over. They may be blue or brown or dark gray. From 500 to 1,500 feet down, the fishes are usually silvery or light gray, and those in the abyss, below 1,500 feet, are almost all black, though some red ones have been found.

Fish from the deep sea, where there is little light, often have large eyes, with pupils which can be enlarged until they are almost the size of the whole eye. Fish from the greatest depths, where there is no light at all, have smaller eyes, since there is no longer any advantage in eye size. Some of them are almost totally blind and depend on feeling organs. Some have their own lights which they carry around with them, both to light the way and to attract prey.

Depth also increases pressure. Every creature on earth has to adjust to pressure. We ourselves bear a weight of fifteen pounds air pressure per square inch of our bodies. We don't realize that air weighs so much because our bodies are pressing outward with the same force.

Water, of course, is much heavier than air, and fish have to stand a pressure that can be anything from fifteen pounds to seven and a half tons per square inch! How do they do it without being squashed flat? The answer is that the pressure within their bodies is the same as that of the water outside them. Besides, most fish have swim bladders containing gases or air, perfectly adjusted to keep them in the zone where they belong.

Of course most fish can move up or down to some

extent, and their swim bladders adjust to the change. However, if a deep-sea fish did try to take a trip to see a cousin up above, the gas in its swim bladder would expand greatly as it moved upward where the pressure was less. This would make the fish so light that it would pop right up to the surface. The lack of pressure there would cause all its tissues to swell up, and it would die from falling upward.

Dr. Smith considered all these facts. He was sure he could do some detective work and make at least a deduction as to where the coelacanth lived when it was at home. Scientists all over the world were speculating about it. Some said the creature was a refugee from the great depths of the ocean and had been caught when a fishing boat trawled deeper than usual. And why had it been living in the depths? It must have gone there to escape the competition of modern fish. Maybe there were other relics of past ages still lurking in the abyss.

Nonsense, said Dr. Smith. He had examined hundreds of fish from the abyss, and they were all descended from modern types. There was evidence that the very deep sea had not been populated at all hundreds of millions of years ago, but that the creatures in it had moved down there fairly recently.

And then, trawlers often fished at 300 fathoms (1,800 feet) and had never caught a coelacanth. This one had been caught at forty fathoms (240 feet).

No, Dr. Smith said, this fish does not live either in the great depths or in shallow water. It is bluish all over, and abyssal fish are black. And it was hauled up on deck in a net full of sharks. It was at the bottom of the heap, and yet it didn't die for hours. A deep-sea fish would have died at once.

Besides, look at its body. It had tough scales, bony plates on its head, strong fins, and sharp teeth arranged in clumps all through its mouth. It must live down among rocks, not too far out from land, but deep enough to escape the surface waves. It would not be able to swim fast for a long distance, but it would not need to. It would lurk among rocks, concealed by its bluish color, and swoop out at any passing fish. And nothing, once grabbed, could escape from those teeth.

The problem was to find a place that corresponded to the requirements of the fish.

As time went on, it seemed less and less likely that it could be anywhere near by. No trawler or line fisherman anywhere along the coast of South Africa could remember catching such a fish. But wait!

Dr. Smith looked at the map. All down the coast of South Africa flows the powerful Mozambique Current. It comes down through the Mozambique Channel, between East Africa and the island of Madagascar. Could that current have washed the coelacanth down from there?

Little was known about the waters off East Africa. The country belonged to the Portuguese. It was wild and tropical, and most of it was still unexplored. The continental shelf plunged steeply away from the coastline, and there were many rocky reefs among which fish could hide. The people of East Africa had always been fishermen. Why had nobody ever caught a coelacanth?

Well, maybe someone had. It was possible that the natives caught them all the time, but in places so remote that the news never reached civilization. It could be, too, that the fish lived in waters so wild that nobody could fish there at all.

Then there was that enormous island of Madagascar, with its 3,000-mile coastline. Fossil coelacanths had been found there. Why not live ones?

Dr. Smith felt sure that if he could only search the waters between East Africa and Madagascar, he would find more coelacanths. But how could he do

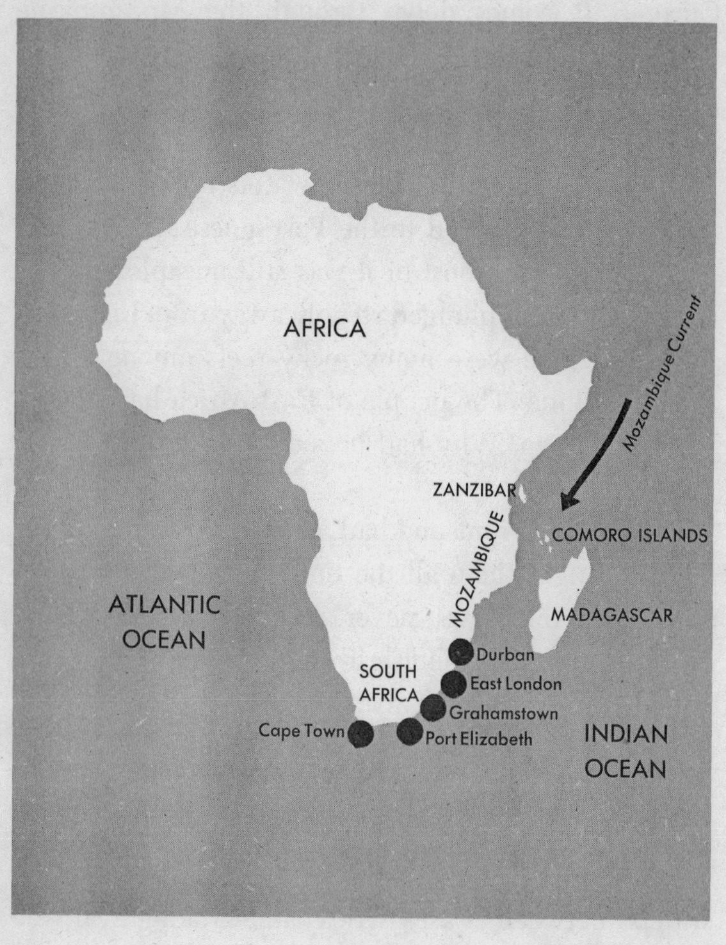
AFRICA
Mozambique Current
ZANZIBAR
MOZAMBIQUE
COMORO ISLANDS
MADAGASCAR
ATLANTIC
OCEAN
Durban
SOUTH
AFRICA
East London
Grahamstown
Cape Town
Port Elizabeth
INDIAN
OCEAN

that? He was not young, he was not rich nor influential. Besides, the world was on the brink of war once more, and that overshadowed everything else.

Still, he did not give up hope. Pictures of the coelacanth were sent to all fishing boats. Rewards were offered. Dr. and Mrs. Smith talked to everyone they met.

In 1940, the monograph on the first coelacanth was published. As he held the book in his hand, he resolved that, come what might, he would somehow get another specimen.

Chapter 6

Captain Hunt

AND NOW WORLD WAR II darkened the world. For five long, sad years, fighting was more important than anything else — certainly more important than fish. Dr. Smith was very busy teaching chemistry, for chemists must be trained to make explosives. But he waited for the day when he could forget all this and get back to his beloved fish.

In 1945 the war ended and the research he longed to do became possible. Money was raised by the South African Council for Scientific and Industrial

Research, and he was asked to write a book about South African fishes. He had always wanted to do this. In fact, he had made a start on it years before, but had never had the means to devote his whole time to it. Now he could do so. He resigned from the chemistry department.

Then a new life began — a life of research, of trips up and down the coast to collect specimens, of exploring in wild, jungle-covered places, of talking with fishermen, and, best of all, of working in his own laboratory.

And always in his mind was the coelacanth. He would have liked above all to organize an expedition to find one, but he had no money for that. However, there was one thing he could do. He had leaflets printed in English, French, and Portuguese, showing a picture of the fish and offering a reward of a hundred pounds to anyone who found one. The leaflets were distributed far and wide, especially in East Africa and Madagascar, for he was convinced that the home of the coelacanth must be somewhere in that region.

The native fishermen thought he must be crazy to be willing to pay so much for a fish. He wasn't discouraged, however, but talked to everyone he met, hoping to find a clue. Only once, in 1948, did he meet a man who said that he had caught such a fish. It was big and oily, the man said, and the flesh was soft; so was the skeleton. The scales and the fins looked like the ones in the picture on the leaflet. He had caught the fish one evening, in deep water, off an island. But which island, he could not remember.

The book on South African fishes was published in 1949. It was a beautiful volume, filled with pictures of gorgeous fishes of every shape and color. He was proud of his work. He didn't expect it to be a very popular book. But to his surprise it was a great success, and the first edition was soon sold out. People in South Africa really were interested in fish!

As soon as the book was published, the Smiths went off on more expeditions. In 1950 and 1951 they explored the coast of Mozambique, a wild place with an enormous reef. It was a fish collector's paradise. All kinds of marvelous fish swarmed there — millions of them, so unused to humans that they almost jumped into the nets.

It was a difficult place for the humans, though. There were islands covered with prickly bushes but no fresh water. There were no supplies; everything had to be carried along. It was very hot, and there were man-eating lions in hordes. The lions liked a native for dinner now and then, and it was horrible to hear screams at night as they tore open native grass huts in search of human prey.

But there was no sign of a coelacanth, and indeed Dr. Smith's fellow scientists thought him mad to suppose that there might be any along this coast. In fact, as he went north, he himself was beginning to be worried. He was coming to the place where the Mozambique Current started. Beyond this, it branched off to the north, and if the coelacanth had been washed south by it, the fish's home must be around here somewhere. Then why couldn't he find it?

As he sailed up and down the coast in his little boat, he looked across the channel to Madagascar. He would have liked to search there. But the Madagascar coast was 3,000 miles long. It would take years to explore it. Besides, the French had a scientific institute there, and if a coelacanth had been found, he would surely have heard of it.

Anyway, he had another hunch. In the channel was a cluster of little islands, the Comoros. He knew almost nothing about them, except that they belonged

to France and were covered with high mountains. He had never seen them, except on maps. Every time he planned a trip, those little dots in the sea fascinated him, and often from his boat he looked across the water and wished he could go there. But they were 200 miles off the coast of East Africa, and he had no compass in his small boat. And his wife and crew were distinctly unenthusiastic.

In 1952 the Smiths were working in Zanzibar. Just before they left there, they held an exhibition, so that the local people could see the things they had collected. Crowds came — not just those who were merely curious, but fishermen who were interested from a professional point of view.

Mrs. Smith always made it her business to circulate among these people and talk to them, for she got much useful information that way. On this day she noticed a tall, handsome stranger reading one of their leaflets telling about the coelacanth, and she went up to him and asked if he had ever seen such a fish.

No, he had not, but he was interested. His name was Eric Hunt, and he was the captain of a small schooner in which he fished and traded between Africa and the Comoros.

The Comoros! At the word, Mrs. Smith pricked up her ears. She told him how interested her husband was in the islands. She told him all about their search and explained why the fish meant so much to Dr. Smith. She gave him a pile of leaflets, and Captain Hunt promised to distribute them. He would let them know if he ever heard of a coelacanth's being caught.

The Smiths went on with their expedition, and on the way home they stopped at Zanzibar again. Again they met Captain Hunt, who had just come back from the Comoros. He reported that he had showed the leaflets to the French governor there. The governor was very much interested, and had had the leaflets sent all over the islands by native messengers. It would be a fine thing, said Captain Hunt, if one of their people should catch such a fish and get the reward!

Then he asked what he should do if he did get a coelacanth.

"Preserve it in formalin," said Mrs. Smith. "You would need quite a lot, because it is a very big fish."

"But what shall I do," he went on, "if I can't get any formalin? There's no refrigeration in the Comoros, you know."

Mrs. Smith shuddered. "Don't even think of such a horrible thing," she said.

"But really," he persisted, "I ought to know what to do."

Mrs. Smith remembered that the natives were in the habit of preserving sharks for food by salting them. In fact, the smell, close to the salting works, was almost unbearable.

"Rub salt in it, the way the natives do," she said.

"All right," said Hunt, laughing. "And if I catch one, I'll send you a cable."

The Smiths were ready to go home. They had almost a hundred boxes of preserved specimens. They went on board their ship, the *Dunnotar Castle,* and sighed with relief. They were tired, and it would be good to rest. Dr. Smith looked forward to getting home.

"It will be a long time before anything gets me back to the tropics again," he said.

He was to remember those words.

Chapter 7

The Second Coelacanth

IT WAS THE DAY BEFORE CHRISTMAS, a lovely warm, clear day. Early that morning the *Dunnotar Castle* docked at Durban, on its way south to Grahamstown. Dr. Smith was happy and relaxed. He had had a successful trip. The hold was full of specimens. Soon he would be back in his laboratory, doing the work he loved. He had not found a coelacanth, but otherwise life was very good.

Friends came aboard to visit with the Smiths. Newspapermen came in search of stories.

As they sat talking, a young ship's officer handed Dr. Smith a telegram. He took it and went on talking. He had received a good many telegrams that morning, and this was probably just another request for advice. After a while he got around to opening it.

He stared at the words. He could not believe his eyes. What he saw there was incredible. He sat as if frozen.

His wife jumped up, frightened at the shock she saw in his face. "What's the matter?" she exclaimed.

"Hunt's got a coelacanth!" the professor stammered.

Mrs. Smith seized the telegram from his hand and read it quickly.

> REPEAT CABLE JUST RECEIVED HAVE FIVE FOOT SPECIMEN COELACANTH INJECTED FORMALIN HERE KILLED 20TH ADVISE REPLY HUNT DZAOUDZI.

It had been sent to the University at Grahamstown. Someone there had sent it on to Durban.

But where in the world was Dzaoudzi?

"I can find out," said the young officer, and he ran off. In a few minutes he was back. Dzaoudzi was a tiny place on the little island of Pamanzi, in the Comoros.

So he had been right! It *was* the Comoros! But what was to be done now? If it hadn't been so difficult, it would have been funny. A few days ago the Smiths had been practically on the spot. They had been glad to leave. Now they would have given anything to be back there.

This was the 24th, and Hunt had already been waiting four days for an answer. The weather in the Comoros was hot as a furnace, and there was no refrigeration. Why did these things have to happen at Christmastime? It was the 1938 story all over again — everyone on vacation, communications difficult, and no transportation available.

The professor would have to get to the Comoros. But how? There were no boats going that way. Even if there were a boat, it would be too slow. It would have to be a plane. But there were no planes either. No airlines had planes going to East Africa, and he certainly didn't have the money to charter a private plane.

The Smiths tried to think of some alternative. Their friends, scientists who understood the situation, gathered around. Were there any men in Madagascar who could take care of the fish until Smith could get there? There was Dr. Jacques Millot, who had been at a conference with Dr. Smith a short time ago. He was the greatest French authority on fish. But he was back in

Paris, and as far as they knew there was no other ichthyologist anywhere near.

A plane was the only answer, cost what it might. One of their friends went off to see if there were an airline in Durban that would be willing to send one. But he soon came back to say that no plane was to be had.

Meanwhile Smith sent a cable to Hunt:

IF POSSIBLE GET TO NEAREST REFRIGERATION, IN ANY CASE INJECT AS MUCH FORMALIN POSSIBLE CABLE CONFIRMATION THAT SPECIMEN SAFE. SMITH.

Then he paced the deck, trying to think of some way to solve the problem. The fish was 2,000 miles away; it was torrid weather; there was no way of knowing whether Hunt had enough formalin to preserve so large a fish; and worst of all, there was the nagging thought that maybe it was not really a coelacanth.

The only way to find out was to go and see for himself, and the only way to get there would be to get the use of an army plane through someone high up in the government, maybe the Prime Minister himself. And then, if it turned out not to be a coelacanth, but some old dead rock cod, how foolish he would feel!

Well, there was nothing to do but try. But he wouldn't try the Prime Minister first. Once before he had asked help of a prime minister and had been rebuffed.

It had happened several years ago, when a great eruption of undersea volcanic gases had killed millions of fish, and hundreds of rare specimens were being washed up on the coast. It was the kind of thing an ichthyologist may see perhaps once in a lifetime. Dr. Smith had had no way to get to the spot and had appealed to Dr. Smuts, who was then Prime Minister, to authorize the use of a plane. Dr. Smuts had not even deigned to see him. A prime minister has almost the status of a king in South Africa, and Dr. Smith was too proud to risk another rebuff now, if he could avoid it. Besides, this prime minister, Dr. Malan, was old and set in his ways. He probably would not be in the least interested in an obscure fish several thousand miles away.

The first thing was to try some of the cabinet ministers. The Smiths went into action on the telephone.

But the first minister they tried was in the United States. The second was on vacation in Cape Town. The Minister of Transport was not to be found anywhere. The Minister of Defense was on his farm, miles from the nearest telephone.

"Heaven help South Africa," thought Dr. Smith, "if we should be suddenly attacked!"

Christmas Day arrived, but Dr. Smith was too tired and worried to eat the Christmas dinner that was put in front of him. He was exhausted, but he couldn't sleep. The ship would not stay in Durban forever. It would weigh anchor in another day or two, and what was he to do?

The day after Christmas, the post office located the head of one of the armed services. Dr. Smith began to explain his predicament.

The man broke in. "Do you mean to say you're interrupting Christmas holidays on account of a fish!" he shouted. "Why, I could not do anything for you without the consent of the whole Cabinet!"

Smith was desperate. But now a new emergency arose. Another cable arrived from Captain Hunt:

CHARTER PLANE IMMEDIATELY AUTHORITIES TRYING CLAIM SPECIMEN BUT WILLING LET YOU HAVE IT IF IN PERSON STOP PAID FISHERMAN REWARD TO STRENGTHEN POSITION STOP INJECTED FIVE KILO FORMALIN NO REFRIGERATION STOP SPECIMEN DIFFERENT YOURS NO FRONT DORSAL OR TAIL REMNANT BUT DEFINITE IDENTIFICATION HUNT.

So now the authorities at the Comoros wanted to take the coelacanth away from him. This was too much! It was his fish. He alone had distributed thousands of leaflets. He alone had insisted that it must live somewhere off the coast of East Africa. He had searched for fourteen long years. Yes, he would apply to the Prime Minister. He would move heaven and earth.

From the home of Dr. Shearer, a member of Parliament, a telephone call was put through to Dr. Malan's summer home. It was evening. They sat around the table listening, while Dr. Shearer talked. He was explaining to someone that they must get through to the Prime Minister. It was a very important matter. They would not bother the Prime Minister otherwise.

But strict orders had been given that Dr. Malan was not to be disturbed. It was impossible. Smith's heart sank. Then Dr. Shearer talked to Mrs. Malan. He was telling her the whole story. The professor felt a twinge of hope. Then despair again. No, said Mrs. Malan, her husband could not be disturbed. He was in bed. He was very, very tired. She would tell him in the morning.

The company sat around the table, dejected and

hopeless. The morning would be too late. Tomorrow the ship was to proceed, and the Smiths would be on board. The fish might as well be given to the French or thrown away, for all the good it would do. It was no use.

Suddenly the telephone rang. Everyone jumped. It sounded like a fire alarm in the stillness.

Dr. Shearer jumped to the phone. He spoke a few words. Then he shouted: "Quick, Professor — Dr. Malan! Dr. Malan wants to speak to you!"

Smith seized the phone. A woman's voice spoke to him: "Mrs. Malan here, Professor; the Doctor wants to speak to you."

And then a deep voice said, "Good evening, Professor. I have heard something of your story, but will you please give me as full a summary as possible."

The professor began to explain. He talked on and on. He read the cables from Captain Hunt.

At last Dr. Malan said he understood the importance of the matter. Something would be done at once. He himself would get through to the Minister of Defense. He would give orders for a plane to be put at the professor's disposal to take him where he wanted to go.

Dr. Smith put down the receiver. He was dazed. He could hardly believe his good fortune. What had caused the change? He didn't know. Much later he learned the whole story. Dr. Malan had heard his wife talking on the phone and had insisted on knowing who wanted him. When she told him, he said, "This man Smith is well known. Bring me that fish book."

She had brought him Dr. Smith's book on the fishes of South Africa, which had been sent to him as a gift. He read over the pages on the coelacanth slowly, and then said, "The man that wrote this book would not ask my help at a time like this unless it was desperately important. I must speak to him now."

Chapter 8

A Wild Flight

AND NOW THE PROFESSOR went into high gear. There was not a minute to be lost.

He and his wife hastened back to the ship. There were specimens to be taken care of. Mrs. Smith had to be instructed about caring for them when they got to Grahamstown.

Dr. Smith would need supplies for his trip. He told his wife to go to bed and get some rest, but he himself sat up all night, planning, making lists, packing.

As soon as it was light, he was up and out. Supplies

had to be dug out of the luggage in the hold. A traveling stove, cooking utensils, and tools were needed, as well as rain gear, flashlight, camera and films, medicines, and cigarettes. The professor didn't smoke, but he had found that there was nothing as effective as cigarettes for winning his way in strange places.

Food had to be collected — cheese, dried fruit, nuts, biscuits, and other things which would not spoil and would be nourishing in case of emergency, for he had no idea where he might have to land.

He needed gallons of formalin, but it was a Saturday and no factories were open. No drugstore had that much. A friend went to the owner of a factory and persuaded him to go to his plant and get the formalin.

He had to get money — 200 pounds in East African currency, and 500 pounds more to use in case of emergency.

The ship was to sail at 11:30 A.M. His wife would be on it. But there was still no news of the plane that was to take him to the Comoros. What had happened to it? Time was passing, and Mrs. Smith did not like to go off, not knowing whether her husband would leave for East Africa that day or the next, or whether something had happened to cancel the whole adventure.

What had happened was that Dr. Malan had not been able to get through to the Minister of Defense. There had been violent storms and the telephone lines were down. At last Malan had sent a policeman by car over the worst kind of roads to take the message.

Sailing time came. Dr. Smith said good-bye to his wife and went ashore. He watched as she stood on the bridge waving and the crew loosened the ropes. The ship steamed off, out of the harbor.

Now there was nothing to do but wait. Dr. Smith went to the house of his friend Dr. Campbell, to try to get some rest. But there was no rest for him. All he could do was pace the floor and listen for the telephone.

At last the word came. A big army passenger plane, a Dakota, was being made ready, and would leave the army base next morning, before dawn. It would get to Durban by 6 A.M. At last Smith could relax a bit. He was really going. He sent a cable to his wife and another to Hunt telling him to hold on, that the government was sending a plane.

At midnight, the professor went to bed. At three in the morning he was up. It was a dark, foggy morning. Dr. and Mrs. Campbell had coffee and fruit ready for him. The fruit that he could not eat they thoughtfully

stowed in his bag. The army car arrived, and they took off for the airport. The plane was circling overhead when they arrived. They could hear it but could not see it in the fog.

Then the big Dakota landed. The door opened, and out came six enormous air force officers. Their Commandant, J. P. D. Blaauw, put out his hand.

The professor looked up at the officer towering over him.

"I bet," he said, "when you joined the South African Air Force you never expected to command a plane sent to fetch a dead fish."

The Commandant grinned down at the slight, excited, tousle-haired scientist. It was easy to see that that was just what he had been thinking, and he was glad the professor had a sense of humor.

"Are you ready, sir?" he asked.

"Certainly," the professor told him. "But are you?"

To the surprise of the men, he began to check off food and water. They had standard rations for a short flight and three gallons of water.

That would never do, the professor said. They might be forced down in East Africa. Had any of them ever been there? If not, they had no idea what it would be like in that waterless jungle. He wouldn't leave until they got a five-gallon tank of water.

At last, at 7 A.M., they took off into the fog. The steel hull of the big military plane was not lined. It rattled and echoed to every sound. They had to shout to make themselves heard. Dr. Smith asked what their route would be.

The plan was to land at Mozambique and spend the night there. They had no idea whether they could land on the Comoros or not. Perhaps they would have to go on to Madagascar. They would try to telephone from Mozambique, to see if there was a landing strip on the Comoros.

The professor passed around biscuits, figs, cheese, and litchi nuts. He himself longed for a cup of coffee. He wanted to light his primus stove to make coffee for everyone, but Commandant Blaauw was horrified at that idea. Dr. Smith didn't try to argue with him, though he had cooked safely over a primus in a small boat, rocking on the waves, surrounded by gasoline and TNT.

"Better take a nap, sir," said Blaauw. But Dr. Smith couldn't sleep. He was too excited, too anxious.

The men were amused. Why was he so uneasy? He explained. The fish might not prove to be a coelacanth after all. At this they were shocked. Why, this flight was costing forty pounds an hour! This would be an expensive fish.

They set down at Lumbo, Mozambique, for the night. Nobody there could tell them whether there was a landing field on the Comoros. Couldn't they telephone? No, it was Sunday. The phones didn't work on Sunday.

They had dinner and went to bed at the hotel. It was as hot as the inside of an oven. Smith tossed and turned. What would the Comoros be like? Even hotter. He couldn't sleep, so he got up and wandered about. In the kitchen of the hotel he found some pineapples, bananas, and papaws. He packed some in a box for the rest of the trip and left his card. The manager of the hotel was an old friend and would understand.

At 3:15 that morning they were all up, and at 4:30 A.M. they took off once more. On the ground, it had been hot and steamy, but in the air it was cold. Ahead of them were enormous banks of clouds like red and purple mountains in the dawn. The clouds could mean a storm was coming, for this was the cyclone season.

One of the men brought the professor a bulging gray garment.

"It's going to be very cold up here, sir. You'd better get into this Mae West," he said, holding it out. The original "Mae West" had been a yellow life jacket which could be inflated. It was carried by fliers during World War II, to use in case they were forced down in the ocean, and was named for the well-known plump movie actress. This one was a thickly padded over-all suit.

"You float in this," the officer added, with a grin.

Float! Down there were tiger sharks. A man wouldn't float for more than twenty minutes. But the professor said nothing about that.

They were making for Mayotte, a fairly large island close to the tiny Pamanzi. The pilot kept trying to get Dzaoudzi by radio, to find out if they could land, but there was no answer. They would simply have to circle the islands in the hope of sighting a field.

"But what if a cyclone comes up," said the professor. "What hope do we have?"

"Not much in this wind," said Blaauw. "In the air, we can manage as long as we have fuel enough to get away. On the ground, we would be smashed to pieces, even if the plane were anchored."

They flew on. The professor passed around a kind of fruit salad made of the pineapples, bananas, and papaws he had brought from Lumbo. The men enjoyed it.

"Takes care of us like a nurse," one of them joked.

The professor remarked loudly that coffee would taste good too, but the commandant said nothing. It was plain that he wasn't going to have a stove burning in his Dakota.

Now they were flying over Mayotte. They saw hills and tree-covered valleys — no flat country at all. They could see the huge barrier reef, blue and green, with many coral shoals where all sorts of fish might hide. Someday, thought Dr. Smith, he would come here to collect fish — someday when there was plenty of time.

And now they saw Pamanzi. Yes! There was a tiny airstrip, sticking out into the sea like a thumb. They were going to land. They would have to dive down to sea level and come in from the sea. The professor was so excited that one of the men had to make him sit down and fasten his seat belt.

Down they went, dropping out of the sky onto the earth. The plane bumped over the rough ground and came to a stop just in front of a hill. And all at once, as if nature were trying every trick she had up her sleeve, the rain came pouring down. The roof leaked, and water poured into the plane. The professor rushed to move his sleeping bag and papers. Just as suddenly as it had started, the rain stopped.

People came running. The door opened and in poured a blast of hot air. Smith looked down. There was Hunt, gazing up at him.

The professor felt ready to explode.

"Where's the fish?" he gasped.

Hunt replied, "Don't worry, it's a coelacanth all right," as though he realized Smith's chief anxiety. Then he added, "It is on my boat."

Chapter 9

A Mission Accomplished

IT WAS A GREAT RELIEF to the professor to know that the fish was on Captain Hunt's boat. Mixed up with all the other fears and uncertainties was the thought that the French government might have stepped in and taken the treasure away, as Hunt's cable had warned. In the dark hours of the night, when he could not sleep, Dr. Smith had thought wildly that if anybody did try to take it away from him now, he would get his six big airmen to fight to the death for his right to keep it. In the daylight, he could smile at such wild fancies. Anyway, if it was on Hunt's boat, it was not strictly in French territory.

"Let us go at once and see it!" he exclaimed.

But no, there had to be formalities first. The governor of the Comoros was waiting at his house. They had to go there and be greeted in French, with Captain Hunt acting as interpreter.

There were refreshments on a big table. The Governor and his wife were all smiles and hospitality. But the professor could stand no more.

Could they not go to see the fish and come back for the refreshments later? Of course they could. Everyone jumped into cars and drove to the dock. There lay the schooner at anchor. On the deck was a box, looking like a coffin.

Dock hands and sailors crowded the little wharf and got in the way. Smith wanted to push them aside. But somehow the crowd parted to let him through. The party boarded the vessel. The men lifted the lid of the box. A layer of cotton appeared underneath. Smith was paralyzed. He couldn't touch it. A sailor peeled back the cotton, and there lay the fish. At last, after fourteen years! It was a coelacanth!

The professor was overcome. He laid his hand on the

fish and patted its bumpy scales, and tears poured down his face.

At his request, the men took the fish out of the box so that he could examine it more closely. As Hunt had said, it was different from the first one. There was no first dorsal fin, and the little extra tail was missing. Dr. Smith thought it must be another species, and he decided then and there to name it *Malania anjouanae*, in honor of the Prime Minister of South Africa and the French Island Anjouan, near where it was found.

He took pictures of the fish, and someone else snapped a picture of the entire party. It shows Captain Hunt, the Governor, the airmen, and a crowd of native sailors, all smiling happily, and in the center, with his hand on the fish, Dr. Smith himself. His face is tense with fatigue and anxiety, but full of a great satisfaction.

Commandant Blaauw was nervously watching the sky, and now he insisted that they must get away. It was raining, and the clouds were heavy. If a cyclone struck, they were lost.

Still, they had to go back to the Governor's mansion, where the refreshments were waiting for them. There was a beautiful chocolate cake, but Dr. Smith could not touch it. They said good-bye regretfully. The Governor kindly invited Dr. Smith to come again and stay as long as he liked. Blaauw and Captain Hunt would have liked to sit down and have a long talk, for they recognized kindred spirits in each other. But there was no time.

They hurried off to the airstrip. The box containing the coelacanth had been stowed on the plane. Dr. Smith gave Captain Hunt the reward money and said good-bye. They climbed aboard and took off.

Soon the islands were mere dots below them, and they were up among the enormous, mountainous clouds. It was very cold. Dr. Smith put on his Mae West and tried to rest. But he couldn't sit still. He walked up to the cockpit where the two pilots sat.

Suddenly one of them started writing something. He held the slip of paper out to the professor. Dr. Smith's heart pounded. No! It could not be!

Some French fighter planes, said the message, were flying to intercept them.

"What speed can they do?" he asked.

"Don't know exactly," was the answer. "But they are very much faster than we are."

Dr. Smith's mind was in a turmoil. "Any hope of escaping in a cloud?" he asked.

The men shook their heads. "Radar," they said.

"Well," he said, "I don't know how you chaps feel about this, but I'm not going back. I don't believe they would shoot us down if we refused to turn, but I would be prepared to chance that rather than turn back."

The men burst out laughing. The professor was so keyed up that he had not realized he was being teased.

He grinned and went back to the cabin. He lay down beside the treasure. In his mind, he went over and over the story Hunt had told him about its capture.

Off the East African coast and the nearby islands, the continental shelf plunges steeply down from the shoreline. This means that there is deep water quite close to shore. Thus the natives can catch deep-water fish without going very far out to sea, which would be dangerous in their little canoes made of hollowed-out logs. In these they paddle a little way out and let down long lines with sinkers made of lumps of coral.

On the twentieth of December, a fisherman named Ahmed Hussein, who lived in a tiny village on the island of Anjouan, went out in his boat with a friend. They took some small fish for bait, and then let down their long lines to about thirty fathoms, they said. (Later it was said to be about a hundred fathoms.)

They went at night, because the fishing was always better then.

In the middle of the night, Hussein caught a big fish. He pulled it to the boat. It struggled, and would have upset the boat if he had not beaten it on the head with an oar and killed it. The two men pulled it into the boat and went home. They were so tired that they didn't bother to clean the fish. They just threw it on the ground and went to bed.

Next morning Hussein took the fish to market. He was sitting on the ground, getting ready to cut it up for sale, when the local schoolteacher came along.

"Stop!" he cried. "Don't cut that fish!"

"Why not?" Hussein wanted to know.

"Because you'll get a lot of money for it," the teacher said. "A hundred pounds!"

"A hundred pounds! You're crazy!"

"Look here, man!" The teacher pulled out one of Dr. Smith's leaflets. There was no knowing whether Hussein could read or not, but he certainly could see the picture on the leaflet.

"What shall I do with it then?" he asked.

The teacher advised him to take it to Captain Hunt. By some lucky chance the schooner was anchored on the other side of the island, and the teacher had

learned of this by the local grapevine. It was twenty-five miles over the roughest kind of ground — deep valleys and rugged mountains — to Hunt's boat. Hussein and his friend thought the whole idea was crazy, but then, for a hundred pounds one does crazy things. They hoisted up the fish and started to hike across the island. The heat was terrible, but they kept going. Why the fish didn't rot away on the journey, nobody will ever know.

The minute Hunt saw it, he knew it was a coelacanth.

"You did the right thing," he assured the man. "You'll get the reward."

The men knew Hunt and trusted him. They gave him the fish. But now it was up to him to take care of it. Where could he get formalin? He rushed to the doctor. But the doctor was away. Then he remembered what Mrs. Smith had said about salt.

"I'm going off to get salt," he told his men as he rushed away.

While he was gone, the men, eager to help, began to get the fish ready for salting. They knew about salting fish. What you did was to hack it open down the back. Of course this was for eating, not for science.

When Hunt came back, there was the coelacanth with a deep gash through the head and body. He salted it well, however.

As he worked, he questioned Hussein and his friend. Had they ever seen such a fish before?

"Oh yes!" they told him. "Not very often, but every now and then we get one. Kombessa, we call them. You can't cook them fresh, the meat gets too soft. But we salt them. They're very good salted. We catch them on a line, in deep water, in cyclone time."

Then somebody added that the scales were good for scratching bicycle tires before putting on a patch. The rubber cement would not stick unless the tire was roughened, and these scales were better than sandpaper.

So all these years native fishermen had been eating these priceless fish for dinner and using their scales for sandpaper!

Now Hunt had to act fast. He had to get the news to Dr. Smith. He had to notify the Governor at Pamanzi. He got the formalin from the doctor and injected it into the fish. He had a box, lined with metal, made to hold the fish.

He was somewhat disturbed when no answer came

from the professor, epecially as the news had reached the Scientific Institute of Madagascar. The people there declared that the fish was a scientific treasure of France and belonged to them. Hunt used all his persuasion to get them to say that Dr. Smith could have it if he came for it in person. Perhaps they did not really think he would. If so, they did not know Dr. Smith.

And now the plane landed at Durban. The professor breathed a deep sigh of relief and gratitude. Now, he thought, he would get some sleep and rest up for the next day, when he hoped to present the fish to the Prime Minister. He had made up his mind that nobody would be allowed so much as a glimpse before Dr. Malan.

To his dismay, there were crowds at the airport. There were reporters and photographers. Could they see the fish? Could they have a picture?

"No, no!" cried the professor.

"Well then, will you make a speech?"

Someone pushed a microphone in front of him. He could barely croak.

"But you've got to say something, man," they told

him. "The whole country is waiting to hear from you. Everybody is proud of you."

"But what can I say?" he asked wearily.

"Anything — just a few words, if that's all you can do."

Then he remembered the notes he had made in the plane. They were rough and confused. But the people deserved a report. He got the notes and began to speak from them. Suddenly his weariness left him, and he was telling the whole dramatic story, even to the tears that came when he first saw the fish.

At last it was over, and he could go to bed. A room was ready for him. But where should they put the fish?

Dr. Smith didn't hesitate. He and the fish would not be parted. He would take it to bed with him if necessary. So that night he slept in a real bed, for the first time in many nights, and the fish lay in its box on the floor beside him.

The next morning they were to fly south to Cape Town. From there a car would take them to the home of the Prime Minister.

Before he went to bed, the professor telephoned his wife at Grahamstown. He told her that they would be at Grahamstown at 6 A.M., and asked her to meet him at the airport with coffee, food, copies of his book, *The Sea Fishes of Southern Africa,* a piece of white cloth, a small board, and ten yards of string.

Mrs. Smith was used to strange requests, and did not show surprise, but she did ask whether she could not go along to Cape Town. Special permission had to be obtained for this, as there was a strict rule against letting women ride in military aircraft. But the Brigadier General, wakened at 12:20 A.M., said sleepily that as everything else about this flight had been irregular, he supposed Mrs. Smith might as well go along.

At four in the morning, they were ready to go. At seven, Mrs. Smith came on board at Grahamstown. Coffee and food were served to the party, and the books were presented to the Commandant and officers of the plane.

An hour or so later, as they were flying over Knysna, where the Smiths' eldest son was on vacation, Dr. Smith dropped a parachute, which he had made from the board, the cloth, and the string, with a message for young Smith. It made a perfect landing, but scared the natives out of their wits, for they thought they were being bombed.

A little later Commandant Blaauw suddenly turned to the Professor and, pointing to his earphones, handed him a message.

"Message from Dr. Malan," it said, "he thanks you very much for having taken the trouble to come so far, but he does not wish to see the fish and wishes you a safe return to Grahamstown."

Dr. Smith felt like a deflated balloon. What had happened now? He could not even guess. He tried to hide his disappointment and put the slip of paper in his pocket.

"Oh well," he said, "now we are so far we can lunch in Cape Town and go back early this afternoon."

Then he saw the men laughing at him and realized that they were teasing him once more. At the moment he would have liked to strangle them.

At last they landed and were taken in a car to the home of the Prime Minister. The great moment had come. The box was set down under a tree. Dr. and Mrs. Malan stepped up to it. The Professor lifted the lid.

The Prime Minister peered at the fish. Then he turned to Dr. Smith with a twinkle in his eye.

"My, it is ugly," he said. "Do you mean to say we once looked like that?"

"H'm! I have seen people that are uglier," said Dr. Smith, to whom the fish was a thing of beauty.

He gave the Prime Minister a scale from the fish as a souvenir. There were speeches, refreshments, and crowds of visitors. Flash bulbs went off as press photographers took pictures.

At last the Smiths and their fish were back on board the plane, and flying home to Grahamstown.

The mission was accomplished.

Chapter 10

Le Poisson

At the Comoro Islands, meanwhile, the French were being stirred to action. The foremost ichthyologist of France, Professor Jacques Millot of the Paris Museum of Natural History, arrived to take charge. He gave all possible credit to his colleague, Professor Smith. But it was true that the two specimens the professor had collected were sadly battered. Now there would be a systematic search for coelacanths. Obviously they lived in French territory, and it was up to France to find more — for France and the world.

Leaflets were issued by the Scientific Research Institute of Madagascar. They were distributed by the thousands. A reward was offered for every coelacanth caught. No more coelacanths were to be eaten. In fact, for a while it seemed as if no fish at all would be eaten in the Comoros, for every able-bodied person was using all the fish he caught as bait for coelacanths.

Now that the fish was so famous, the natives of the Comoros admitted that they had always known about it. They had called it Kombessa. Now they called it *Le Poisson*, French for "The Fish."

In September 1953, the third coelacanth was caught. The man who hooked it was a fisherman named Houmadi Hassani, who lived in the ancient town of Mutsamudu on Anjouan Island.

Hassani went out at night in his little boat, a primitive canoe hollowed out of a single log, with two outriggers for balance. The boat was not wide enough for a man to sit in. Hassani sat on the gunwales, cross-legged, and paddled with a flat piece of wood tied to a stick.

He baited his iron hook with roudi, a kind of African catfish, and let it down more than a hundred fathoms. When the fish struck, he thought he had hooked a shark. It was very strong, and fought hard. He played

it for a long time, letting it get tired, and then he saw that he had *Le Poisson.* It was a big fish. It weighed 88 pounds, almost as much as Hassani himself. Could he bring it in undamaged? He decided to try. He didn't beat it on the head, but subdued it with a few pokes of his boat hook. Then he towed it in to shore. He carried it to his house, a two-room hut built of lava blocks in a narrow alley in Mutsamudu. He woke up his wife and told her to take good care of the fish. Then he ran to the local doctor.

The doctor was asleep. He didn't appreciate it when Hassani banged on his door.

"Come quick, I have *Le Poisson!*" he called out.

"Everybody has *Le Poisson* these days," said the doctor. "What does it look like?"

"It's big, with white spots and big shining eyes," said Hassani.

"Go away," said the doctor. "*Le poisson* has no white spots."

He wanted to go back to bed, but Hassani persisted. At last the doctor went with him. One look was enough. It was *Le Poisson.* It did have white spots, and its eyes were large and phosphorescent.

The doctor telephoned to the island administrator, who came at once in the island ambulance. The ambulance was too big to get through the narrow streets to Hassani's house, so they took Hassani's door off its hinges, laid the fish on it, and carried it to the ambulance.

The doctor and the Administrator did not go to bed that night. They injected seven gallons of formalin into the fish. They had the government carpenter build a crate. The mail plane was ordered to wait, and the police cleared the roads so that the ambulance could make a dash to the airport.

Off went the plane with the fish on board. It reeked of formalin and nearly asphyxiated the pilot.

In Madagascar, Professor Millot was waiting. To his great joy, the fish was a fine specimen. The fins were fleshy, but not quite like those of the other two specimens. Dr. Millot was forced to conclude that there is really only one species, but that the individuals vary a great deal. There is therefore no *Malania,* as Professor Smith thought, but only *Latimeria* with individual variations.

Hassani got his reward in the public square of Matsamudu. A hundred pounds (then about $280) was more than he usually earned in three years.

The next fish was caught on January 22, 1954. That was a wild night indeed. At midnight, the Governor of Great Comoro Island was awakened with the news that the fourth coelacanth had been caught. Everybody rushed to the scene. Formalin was injected, a box was built, the fish was rushed to the plane. No sooner was this job completed at four in the morning than a fisherman arrived bowed down under the weight of another coelacanth. They held the plane, went to work, and loaded the second fish on board — and then a third fish arrived!

"We were getting tired of fish!" the Governor commented.

He thought this would go on for quite a while, and

ordered a large supply of formalin. But after that no more were caught for the next ten months.

What Professor Millot really wanted was a live coelacanth. He wished to see the animal in motion, to note how it used its strange fins while swimming, and how it behaved in the water. He offered a double reward for a live specimen.

On November 12, 1954, two fishermen of Mutsamudu were out in their canoe. It was a calm night. The moon had just risen. Suddenly there was a tremendous jerk on the line. The men looked at each other and said, "Kombessa!"

When the fish surfaced, they saw that they were right. Should they try for the double reward? It was a gamble. They ran the risk of losing the fish altogether. They decided to risk it. They did not beat it on the head nor jab it with boat hooks. They pulled it in carefully and slowly, until it was at the boat. Zema, the older of the two men, put his hand into the fish's mouth. He put a second line through the gills, so that there were two lines pulling the fish. Slowly and carefully they pulled the fish to shore, almost a mile through shark-infested waters. They trembled for fear the sharks would devour their prize on the way, but it seemed that by wonderful good luck, the sharks were somewhere else that night.

When they arrived at the dock, the question was how to keep the fish alive. The island Administrator quickly found a whaleboat and had it filled with water, and the fish was put into the boat.

Everybody came out to celebrate. All night the people danced and sang, while the fish swam about in its boat. Its big fins rotated like paddle wheels, its phosphorescent eyes glowed.

But when morning came, the light bothered it. The people put a cover over the boat and poured in fresh water, but the fish got weaker and weaker. It could not stand the heat and the light. It was accustomed to the cold, dark water 100 fathoms down, where the temperature is never more than 54 degrees Fahrenheit. The surface water was 79 or 80 degrees Fahrenheit.

By the time Professor Millot arrived from Madagascar, it was swimming very slowly. Soon it turned on its back, flapped its fins weakly, and died.

And now everybody wanted to catch a coelacanth. An Italian expedition came to Dzaoudzi to take underwater pictures.

The famous French undersea explorer, Captain Jacques-Yves Cousteau, came to the Comoros in his research ship, the *Calypso*. He had a team of aqua-lung divers who went down to explore the shallower water, and he let down automatic flash cameras and thermometers to take pictures and test the temperatures in water too deep for divers. In this way he hoped to learn something about the habitat of *Le Poisson.*

The problem of keeping a coelacanth alive in captivity has not yet been solved.

There are fourteen coelacanths now in museums. No longer do scientists have to wait while thousands of people file by to stare at the big monster from the past. There are now enough for both study and exhibit purposes. They have been dissected and described in great detail. Much has been learned, and much more is yet to be learned.

Chapter 11

The Lesson of the Coelacanth

AND SO THE LONG SEARCH WAS OVER and the dream had come true. What did it all prove?

Well, for one thing, it was one more proof of the theory of evolution.

More than a hundred years ago an English scientist, Charles Darwin, worked out this theory. He had seen in his studies that families of animals are alike in many ways, but that they are also different.

He said they were alike because they were descended from common ancestors. He said they were different because somehow they were able to change enough to survive in changing environments. These changes, he believed, gave rise to new species.

He went even further. He reasoned that man too is, in many ways, so like the lower animals that man himself must be descended from an earlier form.

Darwin did not feel very happy about announcing his theory, for in his day it was believed that every animal was created just as we now see it. But little by little, as more and more proof was found, his version of the story of creation came to be believed.

One proof, as we have seen, is that all living things are made of the same elements. Further proof is that all embryos (young animals before birth) appear to go through stages in which they resemble simpler animals. At one point a chick embryo and a pig embryo both resemble a fish, with gill slits and a tail. In fact, just by looking at the embryos, it would be hard to tell them apart. It seems as if each embryo has to go through the stages that all its ancestors passed through before it is born. Even a human baby, before birth, looks like the embryos of other animals.

Of course the embryos soon lose the parts they will not need. But not all of them. People have muscles that help them move their ears. They have appendixes that are useless remnants of an earlier phase. These vestiges are one more proof of evolution.

Still another proof is the existence of fossils. Darwin was the first to explain them as unsuccessful variations that could not survive and so became extinct. Fossils help to fill in the gaps in the ladder of evolution.

A fossil fringe-fin shows us what fishes were like, back in the great Age of Fishes, 400 million years ago. It shows how it was possible for some of them to climb out on the land and become the ancestors of amphibians. And so we see that some of those lobe-finned, air-breathing fishes were the ancestors of all other vertebrates, all the way up to man, the highest of the vertebrates.

Of course fossils tell us mainly about the bony structure of animals. Scientists who are studying these bony parts can learn much about the soft parts of fossil animals. They can learn even more by examining the embryos of present-day animals.

Now we see what it means to study the coelacanth. We can tell whether some of our previous guesses were right. If the bony structure should turn out to be like that of the fossil fish, it could be assumed that the soft parts would be similar too.

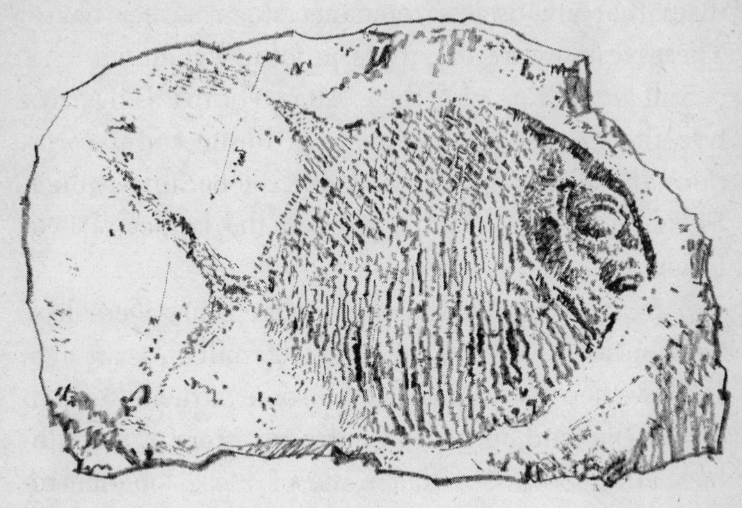

Study showed that *Latimeria's* bony structure was almost exactly like that of the fossil coelacanths. The skull bones are similar. The fins are built like little limbs with bones attached to the shoulder girdle and hip girdle. The scales are similar, fitting into deep sockets and decorated with little knobs. The teeth look the same; they are set in clumps attached to separate plates in the jaws.

It is easy to see the relation between the teeth and the scales. The knobs on the scales are made of strong enamel. Some are smooth, but some are sharply pointed, and all are hollow. The teeth are like scales which have become thicker and stronger, the knobs pointed and sharp.

Latimeria does not have a true spinal column of bone. Instead, its body is supported by a notochord, a long tube, somewhat like a fluid-filled balloon, that extends from the tip of the tail to a hollow in the skull. The ancient coelacanths must also have had a central stiffening structure like a notochord, for the fossils show a space where it would have been.

Now what about the soft parts?

In any vertebrate embryo, the heart begins as a little swelling in the main blood vessel. As the embryo develops, this enlarged part divides into four small compartments. Then the blood vessel bends back like the letter S, and at last the heart becomes a pear-shaped organ with four chambers in the mammal. This takes only a few days in the embryo. Somewhere in the past, our primitive ancestors must have taken millions of years to go through this process. The heart of the coelacanth is so primitive that it is still shaped like the letter S. It is more primitive than any other vertebrate heart.

All vertebrates have a tiny gland, the pituitary, which is very important for growth. In the embryo, the pituitary gland starts as two separate little bulbs, one in the throat and one in the brain. As the embryo develops, they join and become one. But in the coelacanth they can still be seen as a double structure.

The intestine of the coelacanth has an interesting device called a spiral valve. It is shaped something like a tiny spiral staircase. It is not found in modern vertebrate embryos, but it is found in primitive fishes like the sharks. The purpose of this valve is to lengthen the intestine, to slow down the food as it passes through, and to give the body time to absorb all the nutriments. Modern bony fish have a cluster of little pouches attached to the intestine. The higher animals, of course, have long coiled intestines which serve this purpose.

The coelacanth's muscles are strong and very complex, unlike those of modern fish. In a modern bony fish, the important muscles are segments shaped like the letter W. They fit into each other all along the length of the body. In swimming, they contract to bend the body first to one side, then to the other, so that the fish pushes against the water with a swinging motion. The fins are used mainly for steering and for balance. But the coelacanth with its complex fin muscles can rotate its fins in a complete circle, and probably can even creep along the ocean floor with them.

Latimeria is not the only "living fossil" that has been found. There are others that tell us what life was like millions of years ago.

There is a living shellfish called *Lingula*, which is somewhat like a clam and is almost indistinguishable from 600-million-year-old fossils.

There are the crinoids or sea lilies. They look like lovely flowers, but are really related to the sea urchins and starfish, and have survived for 600 million years.

There are the horseshoe crabs, which are not really crabs but are distantly related to the spiders, and which have been on earth for 350 million years.

There are insects that have kept their ancient form. The cockroach, for instance, has remained unchanged for 325 million years.

There is the lungfish, which buries itself in the mud as its ancestors did 300 million years ago.

There are oysters, which look little different on our plates from their ancestors of 200 million years ago.

There is *Sphenodon*, a lizardlike creature which lives on islands off New Zealand and has changed little in 200 million years.

We don't know why these creatures have remained unchanged in their undisturbed corners of the world all these millennia, while other forms have died out. But we are grateful that they have, for they give us glimpses into the otherwise unimaginable past.

Latimeria is important because it represents a point at which life habits changed and led to something different. It is important because it teaches us one more lesson about life, which is the most wonderful thing in all creation.

There is still much that we don't know about the coelacanth: what the young fish looks like, how it reproduces, what its life history is. Someday we shall find out.

INDEX

Index